Derek Jeter

by Kim Covert

Reading Consultant:
Dr. Robert Miller
Professor of Special Education
Minnesota State University, Mankato

CAPSTONE
HIGH-INTEREST
BOOKS

an imprint of Capstone Press
Mankato, Minnesota

Capstone High-Interest Books are published by Capstone Press
151 Good Counsel Drive, P.O. Box 669, Mankato, Minnesota 56002
http://www.capstone-press.com

Library of Congress Cataloging-in-Publication Data
Covert, Kim.
    Derek Jeter/by Kim Covert.
    p. cm.—(Sports heroes)
    Includes bibliographical references and index.
    ISBN 0-7368-0777-2
    1. Jeter, Derek, 1974—Juvenile literature. 2. Baseball
players—United States—Biography—Juvenile literature. [1. Jeter,
Derek, 1974– 2. Baseball players. 3. Racially mixed people—Biography.]
I. Title. II. Sports heroes (Mankato, Minn.)
GV865.J48 C68 2001
796.357'092—dc21   00-009970

Summary: Traces the personal life and baseball career of the shortstop for the New
York Yankees.

Editorial Credits
Matt Doeden, editor; Lois Wallentine, product planning editor; Timothy Halldin,
    cover designer and illustrator; Katy Kudela, photo researcher

Photo Credits
Allsport USA/Rick Stewart, 14; Doug Penfinger, 31; Jonathan Daniel, 35; Vincent
    Laforet, 36; Jamie Squire, 41
AP/Wide World Photos/Doug Mills, cover
Reuters/Jim Bourg/Archive Photos, 4
SportsChrome-USA, 6, 24; Rob Tringali Jr., 9, 10, 13, 17, 18, 23, 26, 28, 32, 38, 42;
    Tony Tomsic, 20

2 3 4 5 6 06 05 04 03 02 01

Table of Contents

CHAPTER 1

A Powerful Home Run

On October 18, 1999, the New York Yankees were playing the Boston Red Sox in the American League Championship Series (ALCS). The Yankees had won three of the first four games in the series. They needed one more win to advance to the World Series.

The teams were playing in Fenway Park in Boston, Massachusetts. The night was cold and windy. The game was on national television. Some of the TV cameras were set up in the center field seats.

Derek Jeter hit a home run in the fifth game of the 1999 ALCS. The Yankees won the game 6-1.

In the first inning, Derek Jeter stepped to the plate to face Red Sox pitcher Kent Mercker. Yankee second baseman Chuck Knoblauch had opened the inning with a single. The count was two balls and one strike. Mercker threw a fastball. Derek swung and blasted the ball deep into center field. The ball sailed through the wind and crashed against the roof above the TV cameras. The 410-foot (125-meter) home run gave the Yankees an early 2-0 lead.

The two runs were all the Yankees needed. They won the game 6-1. The win sent Derek and his teammates to the World Series for the third time in four years. Derek finished the 1999 ALCS with a batting average of .387.

About Derek Jeter

Derek Jeter is the starting shortstop for the New York Yankees. He has been their shortstop since 1996. The Yankees won the

Derek Jeter plays shortstop for the Yankees.

World Series in four of Derek's first five full seasons.

Most baseball experts agree that Derek is one of the best shortstops in baseball today. Some call him the game's most complete shortstop. Derek has speed and power. He hits for a high batting average. He is a good fielder.

Derek also is successful off the field. He is one of baseball's most popular players. He endorses products such as Skippy peanut butter and Nike shoes. These endorsements earn Derek millions of dollars each year.

CAREER STATISTICS

Derek Jeter

Major League Batting Statistics

Year	Team	Games	Hits	HR	RBI	SB	Avg
1995	NYY	15	12	0	7	0	.250
1996	NYY	157	183	10	78	14	.314
1997	NYY	159	190	10	70	23	.291
1998	NYY	149	203	19	84	30	.324
1999	NYY	158	219	24	102	19	.349
2000	NYY	148	201	15	73	22	.339
Career		786	1008	78	414	108	.311

CHAPTER 2

The Early Years

Derek was born June 26, 1974, in Pequannock, New Jersey. He is the oldest child of Dorothy and Charles Jeter. Dorothy worked as an accountant. Charles worked with people who had addictions to drugs and alcohol. He helped them learn to live without using these substances. Derek has a younger sister named Sharlee. Derek's family moved to Kalamazoo, Michigan, when he was 4 years old.

A Childhood Dream

Derek spent many summers with his grandmother. Her name was Dot Conners. She lived in New Jersey. Derek had many cousins who also lived

Derek was born June 26, 1974.

in New Jersey. Many of them were baseball fans. Their favorite team was the New York Yankees.

Dot took Derek to his first major league baseball game when he was 6 years old. Dot and Derek watched the Yankees play at Yankee Stadium in New York.

Derek's father had played baseball in college. He was a shortstop. Charles had saved pictures and newspaper stories about his college baseball games. He showed Derek his baseball scrapbook. Derek wanted to be a shortstop like his father. His dream was to play for the New York Yankees.

A Young Star

Derek showed his baseball talent at an early age. He played in several youth leagues. Charles was Derek's Little League coach.

Derek had many athletic skills. He could run fast. He had a strong arm and could throw the ball far. He also was a good fielder. He played mainly shortstop and second base.

Derek always dreamed of playing shortstop for the Yankees.

Derek played baseball in the Connie Mack League when he was in junior high school. He played for a team called the Maroons. The team included the best baseball players in Kalamazoo. Derek was one of the best players on the team.

A Family Goal
The Jeter family worked together to help Derek improve his baseball skills. They lived next to

A Hero's Hero

Dave Winfield

Derek watched many players as he grew up. He enjoyed watching star shortstops such as the Cincinnati Reds' Barry Larkin. But Derek's favorite player was outfielder Dave Winfield. Derek hung a poster of Winfield in his room.

Winfield had been a star athlete in many sports. He had been drafted by professional baseball, football, and basketball teams. Winfield chose to play baseball. He began his career with the San Diego Padres in 1973.

Winfield played for six major league teams. He played for the Yankees from 1981 to 1990. Winfield was named to the All-Star team 12 times. He hit 465 home runs in his career. He had 3,110 career hits. Winfield retired from baseball in 1995.

the high school baseball field. The family often climbed the fence to practice on the field. They would hit ground balls for Derek to field. Derek also practiced hitting to his parents and sister.

Charles and Dorothy had strict rules for their children. They made sure Derek and Sharlee did well in school. They also taught their children good manners. They would not let Derek play baseball if he did not follow these rules.

Charles and Dorothy also made Derek and Sharlee sign a contract each year. This agreement listed their goals in school and athletics. The contracts helped Derek learn to set and reach his goals.

High School

Derek played shortstop for Kalamazoo Central High School's baseball team. Don Zomer was the coach. He noticed that Derek was the first player on the field for practices and the last one off. Derek often asked Zomer to hit him ground balls. Zomer also noticed Derek's athletic talent. Derek threw the ball so hard from shortstop that Zomer had to change first basemen. The team's original first baseman could not handle Derek's fast throws.

Derek was an outstanding high school baseball player. During 11th grade, his batting average was .557. He batted .508 in 12th grade. The Michigan High School Coaches' Association named him the 1992 Player of the Year. He also earned the Gatorade Award. This honor is given to each state's top high school student-athlete. Winners of the award must be both top athletes and top students.

Education was important to the Jeter family. Derek was an honor student in high school. His parents wanted him to attend college. After graduation, he planned to attend the University of Michigan. He wanted to play for Michigan's baseball team.

Derek has always been among the best players on his team.

The Draft

Many major league scouts watched Derek play during high school. The scouts were deciding whether major league teams should draft Derek when he finished high school. The scouts noticed Derek's speed, quickness, and strength.

Dick Groch was a scout for the Yankees. He called the Jeter family two days before the draft. He said that the Yankees were interested in Derek. The Yankees had the sixth draft pick. On June 1, 1992, the Yankees selected Derek with that pick.

The Yankees offered Derek $700,000 to join their organization. They agreed to pay for his college education. Charles and Dorothy believed that it was important for Derek to go to college. They wanted him to be prepared for his future after baseball. Derek accepted the Yankees' offer.

Derek's dream to play for the Yankees came true when they drafted him in 1992.

CHAPTER 3

The Minor Leagues

Derek began his professional career in the minor leagues. He reported to the Yankees' Gulf Coast League team in Tampa, Florida. He was only 18 years old. It was his first time living away from his family.

Professional Beginnings

Derek did not have a good season in Tampa. He did not hit the ball well. His batting average was only .202. Derek also played poorly in the field. He made 21 errors in 58 games.

Major league scouts noticed Derek's speed and quickness.

Derek was homesick. He missed his family and friends in Michigan. He called his parents every night. He told them how badly he was playing. They encouraged him and told him to keep trying.

Later that year, the Yankees moved Derek to their Class A team in Greensboro, North Carolina. He played the final two weeks of the season there. Derek returned to Greensboro for the 1993 season.

Derek played much better in 1993. He played 128 games for Greensboro. His batting average was .295. He hit 14 doubles, 11 triples, and five home runs. He had 71 RBIs. He also stole 18 bases. The South Atlantic League named him their Most Outstanding Major League Prospect.

Derek was still struggling on defense. He made 56 errors that year. But baseball experts saw that he had the ability to be a great player. *Baseball America* magazine named him the minor leagues' most exciting player.

Derek worked on improving his defense while in the minor leagues.

Derek played his first major league game in 1995.

Minor League Player of the Year

In the spring of 1994, Derek played for the Yankees' Class A team. This team also was located in Tampa. He batted .329 in 69 games. In June, the Yankees moved him to their Class AA team in Albany, New York. There, he batted .377 in 34 games. In July, Derek was named Eastern League Player of the Month.

The Yankees moved Derek up to their Class AAA team in Columbus, Ohio. Derek batted .349 in 35 games there. He also had nine triples and 45 RBIs.

That season, Derek made only 25 errors in 138 minor league games. His total batting average was .344. *Baseball America*, *The Sporting News*, *USA Today*, *Baseball Weekly*, and *Topps* all named him the Minor League Player of the Year.

The Youngest Yankee

In 1995, the Yankees decided that Derek could use one more year in the minor leagues. They did not want to push him too quickly. They signed Tony Fernandez as their starting shortstop. Derek returned to the Class AAA team in Columbus.

In late May, Fernandez injured his ribs. The Yankees needed Derek to take over for Fernandez. Yankee officials told Derek to meet the team in Seattle on May 29. Derek was only 20 years old. He would be the youngest player in the American League.

Derek had reached his childhood goal. He called his parents to tell them that his dream had come true. He was about to play shortstop for the Yankees.

First Major League Games

Charles flew to Seattle, Washington, to watch Derek play in his first major league game. Dorothy stayed home to watch Sharlee play shortstop for her high school team. Derek understood that Sharlee's game also was important.

Derek's first game did not go well. He had no hits in five at-bats. Seattle won the game 8-7 in 12 innings. But Derek did play well at shortstop.

Derek was the Yankees' starting shortstop in the next 13 games. He made two errors and batted .234. On June 12, Fernandez was well enough to rejoin the Yankees. Derek then returned to Columbus.

The Yankees planned to make Derek their starting shortstop in 1996.

CHAPTER 4

The Major Leagues

Derek played for Columbus until September 1995. In September, baseball rules allow major league teams to add more players to their rosters. The Yankees brought Derek back to New York. Derek had only one more at-bat that season. He hit a double that scored a run in a 5-4 Yankee victory over the Milwaukee Brewers.

Joe Torre was the Yankees' manager. He wanted Derek to start as shortstop in 1996. But Torre did not want Derek to feel too much pressure. Derek was still young and

Derek immediately impressed baseball fans with his hitting skills.

inexperienced. Torre placed Derek ninth in the batting order. He wanted Derek to focus on defense.

Opening Day

On April 1, 1996, the Yankees played their first regular season game. Dorothy went to Cleveland to watch Derek play. Charles stayed home to see Sharlee's softball opening game.

Derek began the season strongly. In the fifth inning, he smashed his first major league home run into the left field seats. The home run gave the Yankees a 2-0 lead. Derek also made an important defensive play in the seventh inning. Cleveland shortstop Omar Visquel hit a fly ball into left field. Derek ran into left field with his back to home plate. He watched the ball sail above him. He dived and caught the ball over his shoulder. The Yankees won the game 7-1.

A Championship Season

Derek continued to play well throughout the 1996 season. On July 3, he had his first

**The Yankees faced the Baltimore Orioles in the
1996 ALCS.**

four-hit game. Fans began to notice the young
shortstop. Derek finished fourth in the All-Star
voting for shortstops.

Derek played even better in the second half
of the season. He batted .350 after the All-Star
break. His performance helped the Yankees
win the division championship.

The Yankees faced the Texas Rangers in the
first round of the playoffs. Derek had three hits

The Yankees beat the Orioles to advance to the World Series.

in the second game of the series. He also scored the winning run in the 12th inning. The Yankees went on to win the series. Derek batted .412 in the series.

The Yankees played the Baltimore Orioles in the ALCS. In the first game, Derek hit a long fly ball into right field. It looked like Orioles' outfielder Tony Tarasco might catch it. But a 12-year-old boy reached out from the stands and caught the ball. The umpire said that the hit was a home run. The Orioles were not happy with the call. The Yankees went on to win the game and the series. Derek had a batting average of .417.

The Yankees next played the Atlanta Braves in the World Series. Atlanta won the first two games easily. Both games were in New York. But the Yankees were not ready to give up. They won the next three games in Atlanta to take a 3-2 lead in the series. The teams returned to New York for the sixth game. The Yankees took an early 3-0 lead. They held on to the lead for a 3-2 win. The Yankees were the World Series champions.

Derek ended the 1996 season with a .314 average. He hit 10 home runs and 25 doubles. He was named the American League Rookie of the Year.

Working to Improve
Derek and the Yankees played well again in 1997. Derek batted .291 with 10 home runs.

The Yankees won 95 games and made it to the playoffs for the third straight year. But they lost to the Cleveland Indians in the first round of the playoffs.

Derek worked to improve his game after the 1997 season. He worked out with weights. Weight training gave Derek more strength. He added 15 pounds (6.8 kilograms) of muscle by the beginning of the 1998 season.

Gary Denbo helped Derek improve his swing. Denbo was the Yankees' hitting coordinator. Derek knew how to hit an inside pitch into right field. He also could extend his arms to drive an outside pitch into left field. Many pitchers threw him inside fastballs. He wanted to learn how to extend his arms and pull these balls. He could then drive them into left field. Denbo helped him learn this skill.

The Greatest Season

Derek's weight training paid off in 1998. He hit 19 home runs that season. His batting

The Yankees defeated the Indians in the 1998 ALCS.

average increased to .324. He also improved his play in the field. Derek made only nine errors in 159 games. He made the American League All-Star team. After the season, he finished third in the American League Most Valuable Player Award voting.

The Yankees won 114 games during the regular season. This number was the second highest number of games ever won by a major

league team. The Yankees easily won their first playoff series against the Rangers. Next, they played Cleveland in the ALCS.

Derek showed his skills in the first game against the Indians. He singled and scored in the first inning. He then singled and stole second base in the second inning. In the fourth inning, Cleveland's Travis Fryman hit a ground ball into left field. Derek jumped up to make a backhanded catch. He then threw the ball to first base while he was still in the air. His throw beat the runner. Fryman was out. The Yankees won the game 7-2.

The Yankees went on to beat the Indians in the ALCS. They faced the San Diego Padres in the World Series. The Yankees easily won the series 4-0. They were the World Series champions once again.

The Yankees swept the Padres in the 1998 World Series.

CHAPTER 5

Derek Jeter Today

Derek and the Yankees continued their success in 1999. Derek had a .349 batting average for the season. He also hit 24 home runs and had 102 RBIs. The Yankees kept winning as well. They made the playoffs once again. The Yankees defeated the Rangers and the Red Sox in the first two rounds of the 1999 playoffs.

Another Championship

The Yankees faced the Braves in the final World Series of the 1990s. Many people believed that the Braves and Yankees were the best teams of

Derek and the Yankees continued their success in 1999.

the 1990s. They said the winner of the 1999 World Series would be the team of the decade.

The World Series began in Atlanta. The Yankees trailed 1-0 entering the eighth inning. The first three Yankee batters reached base. Derek came to the plate with the bases loaded. He hit a single to left field to score the tying run. The Yankees went on to win the game 4-1. The Yankees won the next three games of the series and were champions again.

In 2000, Derek and the Yankees again advanced to the World Series. There they faced the New York Mets. The Yankees won three of the first four games of the series. In the fifth game, the Yankees trailed 2-1. Derek came to bat in the sixth inning. He hit a home run to left field to tie the game. The Yankees went on to win 4-2. They became the first team in almost 30 years to win three World Series titles in a row. Derek batted .409 in the series. He was named World Series MVP.

Turn 2 Foundation
In 1996, Derek started the Turn 2 Foundation. The foundation raises money for programs that help

Derek and his teammates celebrated another World Series title in 1999.

prevent teenage drug and alcohol abuse. Derek's father quit his job to run the foundation. His mother and sister also help.

Jeter's Leaders is part of the Turn 2 Foundation. The foundation chooses ninth graders from New York schools. Foundation workers talk to the students and help them through high school. The students must keep a B average in school. They also must promise not to use drugs, tobacco, and alcohol. Students who complete the program receive money to help pay for college.

Career Highlights

1974—Derek is born June 26 in Pequannock, New Jersey.

1992—Derek is named Michigan High School Player of the Year; the Yankees choose Derek with the sixth overall pick in the draft.

1993—The South Atlantic League names Derek the Most Outstanding Major League Prospect.

1994—Several sports publications name Derek the Minor League Player of the Year.

1995—On May 29, Derek plays in his first major league game for the Yankees.

1996—The Yankees win the World Series against the Atlanta Braves; Derek wins the American League Rookie of the Year award.

1998—Derek is named to his first All-Star team; he finishes third in the MVP voting; the Yankees defeat the San Diego Padres in the World Series.

1999—The Yankees defeat the Braves in the World Series.

2000—Derek is named Most Valuable Player of the All-Star Game; the Yankees again win the World Series.

Words to Know

addiction (uh-DIK-shuhn)—a dependence on a drug or other substance

contract (KON-trakt)—a legal agreement between a baseball team and a player; contracts determine players' salaries.

endorse (en-DORSS)—to sponsor a product by appearing in advertisements

professional (pruh-FESH-uh-nuhl)—an athlete who is paid to participate in a sport

rookie (RUK-ee)—a first-year player

scrapbook (SKRAP-buk)—a personal book of items such as photographs and newspaper clippings

To Learn More

Dougherty, Terri. *Derek Jeter.* Jam Session. Minneapolis: Abdo, 2000.

O'Connell, Jack. *Derek Jeter: The Yankee Kid.* Champaign, Ill.: Sports Publishing, Inc., 1999.

Pietrusza, David. *The New York Yankees Baseball Team.* Great Sports Teams. Springfield, N.J.: Enslow Publishers, 1998.

Schnakenberg, Bob. *Derek Jeter, Surefire Shortstop.* Minneapolis: Lerner, 1999.

Stewart, Mark. *Derek Jeter: Substance and Style.* Baseball's New Wave. Brookfield, Conn.: Millbrook Press, 1999.

Useful Addresses

Major League Baseball
Office of the Commissioner of Baseball
245 Park Avenue, 31st Floor
New York, NY 10167

National Baseball Hall of Fame and Museum
25 Main Street
P.O. Box 590
Cooperstown, NY 13326

New York Yankees
Yankee Stadium
Bronx, New York 10451

Internet Sites

ESPN.com—Derek Jeter
http://espn.go.com/mlb/profiles/profile/
   5406.html

Major League Baseball
http://www.mlb.com

The New York Yankees
http://yankees.mlb.com/NASApp/mlb/nyy/
   homepage/nyy_homepage.jsp

Index